Praying with

OUR SORROWFUL MOTHER

Reflections on the Seven Sorrows of Mary

FR. JACOB POWELL

Nihil Obstat: Rev. William J. Anton
          Censor Librorum

Imprimatur: Rev. Robert M Coerver
          Bishop of Lubbock
          January 19, 2023

www.salvereginamedia.com

Print Book ISBN: 9781960410139

And when they met her they all blessed her with one accord and said to her, "You are the exaltation of Jerusalem, you are the great glory of Israel, you are the great pride of our nation! You have done all this singlehanded; you have done great good to Israel, and God is well pleased with it. May the Almighty Lord bless you for ever!" And all the people said, "So be it!"

—Judith 15:9–10

May this book serve for the greater glory of God, the veneration of my Blessed Mother of Heaven, and the salvation of souls.

Contents

INTRODUCTION

Mary once said to Saint Bridget, a well-known mystic of the fourteenth century:

> I look around at all who are on earth, to see if by chance there are any who pity Me and meditate on My Sorrows; and I find that there are very few. Therefore, My daughter, though I am forgotten by many, at least do you not forget me. Meditate on My Sorrows and share in My grief as far as you can.

The Blessed Virgin invites us to reflect on her life. In so doing, we reflect on the life of Christ as well. This leads to our fulfillment because in God alone we discover the real joy and unimaginable reward which He desires for each of us. Because the saints pursued God so fervently and relentlessly, they illuminate for us the "narrow" way to heaven. Their examples and insights reveal His splendor and inspire us to pursue the life of heaven while still here on earth. Their actions and dispositions become road maps to heaven. The more intimately we know their prayers and writings, the more clearly we see their spiritual life open before us. Their love for God becomes visible to us as we develop relationships with them through prayer and reading. The love they have for God is proportionate to the depth of their interior life. Their sorrows, joys, writings, miracles, and service allow us to enter more deeply into their interior life and explore new horizons of the richness of the Catholic Faith.

As remarkable as saints are, the Blessed Virgin far surpasses all of them in her singular love and devotion to the Most Holy Trinity. Her interior life is inexhaustibly rich and surpasses all others. Therefore, she remains the perfect example and the Mother to whom we should entrust ourselves for spiritual enlightenment and growth.

The Seven Dolors (sorrows) of the Blessed Virgin Mary are seven windows into her interior life. Although her pure and immense love extends beyond our comprehension, we are edified by glimpses into her complete surrender to the will of God. She most effectively demonstrates God's love for humanity and most appropriately responds to His love in humility. Her seven-fold sorrow opens the door to her Immaculate Heart, allowing us to explore the magnificence of God manifested most clearly in her life.

This book intends to help readers discover new frontiers of their devotion to the Blessed Virgin. The reflections presented illuminate the hidden life of Mary, which is found between the lines of Sacred Scripture and amplified in Sacred Tradition. Because Mary is the preeminent disciple of Christ, her sorrows instruct us how to endure suffering and advance spiritually from them. Her life is a masterpiece of love that makes visible the Divine Beauty of God. Through her sorrows, we draw ever closer to that Divine Beauty for which our souls' thirst.

These reflections are largely based on Father Frederick William Faber's *The Foot of the Cross, or The Sorrows of Mary,* along with my own mental prayers and meditations.

There is an abundance of grace given to those with a devotion to Our Lady of Sorrows and the Seven Sorrows of Mary. Saint Alphonsus identifies four benefits. First, those who, before death, invoke the divine Mother in the name of Her Sorrows will obtain true repentance of all their sins. Second, they will be protected in their tribulations and especially at the hour of their death. Third, Christ will impress on their minds the remembrance of His passion and will reward them in heaven for their devotion. Finally, Christ will place these devout servants in the hands of Mary and give her the graces to do with them as she desires.

Saint Bridget received seven promises to those who pray seven Hail Marys in honor of the Seven Dolors of Mary each day:

1. "I will grant peace to their families."

2. "They will be enlightened about the divine Mysteries."

3. "I will console them in their pains, and I will accompany them in their work."

4. "I will give them as much as they ask for as long as it does not oppose the adorable will of My divine Son or the sanctification of their souls."

5. "I will defend them in their spiritual battles with the infernal enemy, and I will protect them at every instant of their lives."

6. "I will visibly help them at the moment of their death—they will see the face of their Mother."

7. "I have obtained this grace from My divine Son, that those who propagate this devotion to My tears and sorrows will be taken directly from this earthly life to eternal happiness since all their sins will be forgiven and My Son will be their eternal consolation and joy."

Hail, Holy Queen

Hail, holy Queen, mother of mercy, our life, our sweetness, and our hope. To thee do we cry, poor banished children of Eve; to thee do we send up our sighs, mourning and weeping in this valley of tears. Turn then, most gracious advocate, thine eyes of mercy toward us; and, after this, our exile, show unto us the blessed fruit of thy womb, Jesus. O clement, O loving, O sweet Virgin Mary.

Pray for us O holy mother of God, that we may be made worthy of the promises of Christ.

CHAPTER 1

MARY IS UNIQUE

The Sacred Scriptures are filled with treasures that are discovered through prayer and study. Because the verses of the Bible which directly mention the life and experience of Mary are few, many people struggle to acknowledge the depth of her sorrow. However, greater insight into Scripture introduces us to our Mother in new ways and paints a clearer image of the relationship she had with Jesus. Her sorrows are directly related to her deep knowledge of her Son; distinct insight into this knowledge provides the foundation from which we can construct a more accurate understanding of and appreciation for her suffering.

Natural Knowledge

Mothers have a deep knowledge of their children. They are often the first to identify a difference in the behavior of their children. They spend so much time caring for them that they grow accustomed to their ordinary sounds and movements which indicate their internal disposition. A mother is often the first to recognize illness or discomfort because they understand intuitively certain characteristics and habits of their sons and daughters more than anyone else.

Mary enjoyed this same intuition and much more. She is the perfect and sinless mother who is not impeded by sin. Because sin causes wounds, division, and confusion, her sinless soul better comprehends the reality around her. She perceives without obstruction the feelings and needs of Christ. She understood His anguish and turmoil on a level that far surpasses any other.

Prophetic Knowledge

Mary is not an ordinary mother. In addition to her purity, her Son is the Messiah. The Messiah is the "anointed One" of God for whom the Israelites were waiting. Mary is a Jew who would have been taught about the coming Messiah. Various prophecies of the Old Testament reveal the Messiah as a Savior of God's people, a king born in Bethlehem.[1] Isaiah, a great prophet to the Israelites, describes a servant from God who is to suffer greatly for the salvation of others:

> But he was wounded for our transgressions, he was bruised for our iniquities; upon him was the chastisement that made us whole, and with his stripes, we are healed. All we, like sheep, have gone astray; we have turned everyone to his own way; and the Lord has laid on him the iniquity of us all.[2]

Also, when the archangel Gabriel revealed to Mary that she was to give birth to the "Son of the Most High,"

who would rule over an endless kingdom, she understood very well the many prophecies which revealed His
life.[3] She knew she was to give birth to God's suffering
servant. She knew she would suffer with Him. Although
Mary may not have had perfect knowledge of her trials,
she gave her "fiat," her complete submission to the will
of God with sufficient knowledge of what was asked of
her.

Additionally, Simeon, a priest of the temple, revealed directly to Mary the suffering that she would
endure. He told her, "And a sword will pierce through
your own soul also, that thoughts out of many hearts
may be revealed."[4] Many believe that he revealed to her
in much more detail the variety and magnitude of her
sufferings at this encounter.

Divine Maternity

As the branches of a tree spring forth from the same
trunk, so would the abundance of special grace and
privileges of Mary spring forth from her Divine
Maternity. God chose her from all eternity to be the
mother of Jesus. He received our human nature from
her. God fashioned His mother with the qualities, virtues, and grace befitting her essential role. Therefore,
the Immaculate Conception, which affirms that Mary
had no sin from the first moment of conception, is log-
ical and in accord with Sacred Scripture.

God detests sin. Because the Son of God entered
the womb of Mary, took from her human nature, and
submitted Himself to her as an obedient child, it follows

that this woman was prevented from the stain of Adam and Eve. Because she assumes an essential part in the salvation of mankind with direct relation to the birth of Jesus Christ, it follows that she remained sinless even in her conception, not by her own merit, but by God's benevolence. She is the vessel through which God enters the world in human flesh; therefore, she is the purest and most precious vessel made by God and especially for God.

In the third chapter of Genesis, the Scriptures foretell the destruction of evil by the "seed" of the woman.[5] This verse is the first to prophesy the victory of Christ. According to the Hebrew version of this text, the "enmity" between the serpent and the woman is a complete enmity. If Mary were conceived in sin, she would have belonged to the devil at that time. She would not have this total enmity. This biblical evidence, along with several other passages, supports the Immaculate Conception.

Mary conceived her Son by the overshadowing[6] of the Holy Spirit. Through His power, the Son of God became a man. For this reason, the Holy Spirit is the spouse of Mary. For the ordinary Christian, the Holy Spirit is the giver of divine gifts. He is the Divine Friend, the Consoler and Advocate, the "Alpha and Omega of the spiritual life"[7]....What more is He to His spouse? Mary is "full of grace" because of her special role as the Mother of God and her special relationship with the Holy Spirit.

Pope Pius IX noted, in accord with the Fathers and Doctors of the Church, that "this singular, solemn and unheard-of greeting [hail, full of grace] showed that all the divine graces reposed in the Mother of God and that she was adorned with all the gifts of the Holy Spirit."[8] Consequently, she has extraordinary insight into the life of her Son, an abundance of grace to attain the summit of sanctity, and many rewards in the life hereafter. In the light of the Divine Maternity, the Immaculate Conception, and the other Marian dogmata, we must conclude that Mary was given special knowledge and a unique and profoundly intimate relationship with her Son. This relationship is unsurpassed by any other creature.

Union with Christ

As we compare Mary with every other human person, she is most like Christ. Physically, she is most like Him because He receives His Body from her. Part of His genetic makeup is directly from her. In purity, she is most like Him in that neither of them ever committed a single sin. Neither of them was conceived in the sin of Adam. In love, they resemble each other immensely. They complement each other perfectly well. The Sacred Heart of Jesus and the Immaculate Heart of Mary are one heart. Therefore, we should readily admit that Mary must be most like Christ in His virtues, knowledge, and capacity to suffer. This unity between them becomes a significant source of both her unequaled joy and her dreadful sorrow.

The above-mentioned facts are only a glimpse into the several well-founded scriptural and traditional reasons to appreciate the interior life of Mary. These are only some of the reasons Mary is not simply another woman but the disciple of Christ par excellence. Christ honored His holy mother, so let us honor her as well. As her sons and daughters, we are enriched as we enter more deeply into her soul and discover her rich virtues, her insurmountable joy, and her immeasurable sorrows. She reached the heights of sanctity that are unattainable to us. Through a strong devotion to her, she will help us obtain an abundance of grace and virtues which are beyond our reach. Let us embark on this journey of prayer with the guidance and help of Our Lady of Sorrows.

CHAPTER 2

SOURCES AND CHARACTERISTICS OF MARY'S SORROW

Before explaining each of the dolors of Mary, articulating a general knowledge of her sorrow ensures a greater appreciation of all that she endured. Through this knowledge, the bitterness and extent of her anguish rise to the surface. She suffered immensely in her earthly life for many reasons, only some of which are readily obvious. The reasons for her sorrows covered in this chapter and the characteristics of those sorrows ought to be considered with respect to each individual dolor. In other words, this chapter directly applies to all of Mary's sorrow.

Sources

God's Will

Mary is the pinnacle of the creatures of God next to Christ's humanity. She is exalted above all creatures, and her glory in heaven is greater than all the glory of the angels and saints combined. God desired from all eternity to share His infinite majesty in a singular way with this woman to whom He has given all the heavens and earth and all that is in them. However, her glory is in relation to her merits. Although all heavenly reward originates and flows out of Christ's passion, Mary participated in His suffering more completely than all others. Through her cooperation with God's will, she has given Him more glory than any other creature, apart from the humanity of Christ. Consequently, she has always received a hundredfold for her humble acceptance of God's will in all things, and her perfect submission yields immense celestial reward.[9]

One of God's most glorious gifts to us is to allow us to participate in His glory. Saint Albert the Great said, *"That as we are under great obligation to Jesus for His Passion endured for our love, so also are we under great obligation to Mary for the martyrdom which She voluntarily suffered for our salvation in the death of Her Son."* Having willed His Son to be the New Adam, God also willed to have a New Eve. As Eve played a unique and singular role in the sin of Adam, so did Mary play a unique and singular role in the salvation of Jesus through her Divine Maternity and her sufferings. The Father willed for this New Adam and New Eve to endure the complete force of the physical, mental, and emotional effect of the sin of disobedience—death. They experienced the complete horror of it. Christ's death is the only reason for our salvation; however, God has seen fit to allow us to share in that salvific work of Christ.[10]

Christ's death is fully sufficient for salvation; however, our sufferings allow us to resemble Christ when we accept them humbly and unite them to Christ's passion. Mary's queenly and exalted throne in heaven indicates her complete self-abandonment to the will of God. The grandeur of her eternal reward discloses the holiness of her life.

Love for Christ

The measure of our love for another is the measure of vulnerability we have in relation to that person. For example, a husband deeply in love with his wife is affected more severely by her death than the death of another. Our Lady had no sin or impediment between her and God. She was so immaculately united to her Son that she felt what He felt. Her love was not simply that of a natural love between a son and a mother but nearly infinitely more than that. She loved Him perfectly as a mother, as a Christian, and as a servant. He was absolutely everything to her. She had no attachments, no vices, no problems, no imperfections, and no ambitions that lessened or blemished her immaculate love for Him. Her love was complete; therefore, her sufferings were complete.

The saints make clear that suffering is "the great similitude of Christ." Our Lady bears a likeness to Christ that is vastly different from us because she bears the sufferings of Christ in such an integral way. She was an eyewitness to nearly everything He suffered, even internally; she endured it with Him. In the moments when she was not present physically (e.g., Garden of Gethsemane), she was present in spirit. How impossible it must have been for her to unsee the blows, unhear the insults, or unfeel the torments of her dear Son's passion.

Immaculate Conception

Because our Lady never knew sin in any form, she was uniquely the enemy of Satan and the servant of God in a way that no other human person ever was. She is utterly unique from us sinful humans in that she is an island of purity and holiness amid the sea of sinful humanity. Not for a single moment was she ever separated from God. Always and in every moment of her existence, He found in her a soul truly pleasing and truly precious to Him. Our sinfulness desensitizes us in relation to sin and sorrow. Her purity and perfect love only make the dolors exponentially more acute.

Divine Maternity

God has seen fit for this woman to be our mother. As any good mother experiences and endures the pain of her children, all the more, this most perfect mother entered into the depths of human suffering as she fulfilled her beloved role as the Mother of the Savior. "She lived in His Heart rather than her own. His interests were hers. His dispositions became hers. She thought with Him, felt with Him, and as far as might be, identified herself with Him. She lived only for Him. Her life was His instrument to be done with what He willed."[11]

Some may ask, "Why didn't Christ spare her?" Because He loved her dearly. Her sufferings allowed her to be even more intimately united to Christ, share more fully in His death and Resurrection, and continually experience the perfections of higher glory in heaven forever. He loved her too much to forbid her to uniquely share in the depths of His sorrow on earth, which enables her to uniquely share in the heights of His glory in heaven.

Source of Pain for Christ

Although our Lady never committed a sin that added to our Savior's torment, she knew that she was a source of vast suffering for Him. Our Lord's love for her far surpasses His love for any angel and any saint. Christ alone knew the immensity of our Lady's dolors among humanity. This knowledge increased His sorrow immensely. The sufferings of our Lady added to the sufferings of Christ. Because she knew Him so intimately, her realization that she also added to the weight of His cross pierced her soul even more.

Father Faber reflected:

There was not one fresh indignity offered to Him, which did not pierce her soul and make her bleed inwardly. As blows and blasphemies, insults, derision, and rude handlings were multiplied, it seemed at each new violence as if she could bear no more as if the sea of sorrow needed but another drop to break in upon the fountains of her life and wash them away in one terrific inundation. And yet she had to feel that the sight of her broken heart, ever before Him, was more dreadful to our Blessed Lord than the scourging, the crowning, the spitting, or the buffeting. She was made as it were executioner in chief of her own beloved Son.[12]

Our Lady was a treasure of sweetness to our Lord in His earthly journey where He was surrounded by our sins and imperfections. In her, He found consolation and real delight; yet He sees her absolute torment. As our Lady longs to aid us, wipe away our tears, and console us in sorrow, she could not do this for her own Son in the time of His need.

Sin

Various saints have been given the ability to experience the ugliness of sin from a perception much closer to God's than to ours. Some relate a stench to each mortal sin that could exterminate every living thing on earth. Another mentioned the horror of a single venial sin was so great to cause death if God had not intervened. Our Lady knew the terror and evils of sin keenly. More than any of us, she knew the real repugnance of sin. She watched as our Lord was tormented by the countless sins of humanity. The more innocent the victim, the greater the sin. Nobody is more innocent than Christ. What exceeding evil, what unimaginable malice she witnessed as humanity ferociously tore apart our Creator and Redeemer of the world!

Her Children's State

She desires what God desires; she loves who God loves. Therefore, seeing the state of ingratitude and immorality of humanity caused a deeper tear in the depth of our Lady's Heart. Her children are the ravenous wolves causing unknown levels of suffering to Christ. How she suffered seeing our state of depravity. Every sin added to the weight of her Son's cross and widened the gap between sinner and Redeemer.

Characteristics of Mary's Dolors

Consistent

The sorrows of Mary were consistent in two ways. At least from the moment of Simeon's prophecy, but probably from the first moment of the Incarnation, our Lady endured a consistent shadow of suffering over her. As mentioned above, she had insight into the Sacred Scriptures, which referred to the Messiah's suffering. Therefore, she would have lived under the constant shadow of the passion of her innocent Son.

Her sorrows were consistent in their increase as well. She constantly grew in holiness and love for Christ. Her capacity to suffer increased in relation to her growing love.

> The Passion was not a dark end to a bright life, or an obscure sunset after a checkered day and light of gloom, or an isolated tragedy in sixty-three years of common human vicissitudes (changes). It was part of a whole with consistent

antecedents, a deepening certainty of the darkness, but a portion of a lifelong darkness which for years had known, in this respect at least, no light.[13]

Father Faber does not intend to say that Mary had no joy in her life. She had immense joy, which was not mutually exclusive to her sorrow. Her joy increased as she suffered because her strife was a means of greater holiness. Her sorrows became the path by which she was conformed more and more to Christ. Likened to Christ, she produces an interior and priceless joy which does not prevent human suffering.

Rather, Father Faber reinforces the notion that Mary's sorrow was present to her without reprieve for many years. Her remarkable prayer life and purity of heart kept her centered on God at every moment. This unbroken meditation and sensitivity to God's presence allowed for greater familiarity with the impending sufferings of Christ. Her familiarity with His passion made her keenly aware of the magnitude and variety of pain that would accompany those few days that led to the entombment of her Son.

Interior

Mary suffered physically in various ways throughout her life. However, the force of her sufferings was largely internal, mental, and to the depth of her soul. Generally, this form of suffering is considered greater than physical suffering. Physically, anguish is experienced in one particular area of the body. However, interior anguish can be experienced in many degrees and many forms simultaneously. Saint Bernadine of Sienna said, "So great was the dolor of the Blessed Virgin that if it was subdivided and parceled out among all creatures capable of suffering, they would perish instantly." This is only possible by the power of God. She was tormented emotionally, spiritually, mentally, and otherwise in each of her seven sorrows.

Though these sources and characteristics of the sorrows of Mary merely inform us of the true value and enormity of her turmoil, she embraced all of it. She never considered herself before a total submission to the will of God. The Blessed Virgin never counted the cost of her perfect love for Christ. Though it cost her everything, she humbly gave it all. She never surrendered partially or imperfectly in any one of her trials. She opened her heart time and time again as a sword of bitter anguish was plunged into it.

THE PROPHECY OF SIMEON

According to the prescribed law of the Israelites, a male child would be presented in the temple forty days after birth with an accompanying sacrifice. The child was dedicated to God through this presentation. Generally, a lamb or some similar sacrifice was made at that time. For the poor, two turtle doves could be offered in place of a lamb. Although Joseph and Mary offered two turtle doves from their poverty, they brought Jesus Christ, the Lamb of God, who would eventually be the perfect victim sacrificed for the world. Our Lady is the first to offer the Father a perfectly worthy gift—His own Son. She knew this was to give Him away to the will of the Father. Although He came from her, He belongs to the whole world.

In offering her Son at the temple, she was submitting once again to the desires of God, even to the point of offering Jesus to death. Christ will suffer on the cross, and Mary will not be an obstacle between

Him and the Father's will. She will suffer with Him. "A cross is a crown begun. Suffering is dearer to the saints than happiness."[14] In this presentation, she reinforces the absolute surrender of herself that she gave at the Annunciation: "Let it be done to me according to your word."[15] She holds nothing back for herself and does not turn back for even a moment's respite. "For one moment, her will was visible in the mystery of the Annunciation and then it sank down into the deep will of God and was never seen again."[16] She revealed her will to obey God in all things by her words in the Annunciation; she manifested her will in her actions for the remainder of her life.

Mary is the model for all Christians in her complete surrender but also in her gift of her Son to the Father. All gifts we receive belong to God. Everything we are, except our sinfulness, is from God and should be given back to God. The Father offered the most precious gift of His own Son to humanity. Mary is the first of us to offer Him back to the Father.

From this moment on, our Lady could see the seeds of Jesus's death in her daily care for Him. How often she was reminded of the suffering He would endure. Perhaps working with wood produced the image of the cross; perhaps drinking from a cup reminded her of the chalice of death from which He would drink; perhaps a scratch reminded her of the flagellation. When she held His hand, did she already feel the nails? When she kissed His head, did she already see the streams of Blood flowing from the crown of thorns?

Some early fathers agree that Simeon's prophecy was written in shorthand. He explained much of the details of the passion of the Lord to her when he prophesied the sword that would pierce her soul.[17] Perhaps what she did not already know by virtue of supernatural knowledge from God, she was told by the holy priest in the temple. Father Faber remarks, "She could not see either to the right or to the left of that apparition, which like a blood-red sunset, occupied the whole field of sight."[18] Each day of His life was another wave of her death, re-opening the wounds already made in the recesses of her soul; yet she loved, served, and endured all the more. Her sorrow was hidden from the world but always inescapably present to her. Her entire life was this young boy whose impending death was ever nearer.

Injuries and offenses we endure at the hand of another easily turn to resentment and hatred. Often our love grows cold, and our hearts are hardened when others cause us pain. The Holy Virgin did not succumb to such weakness. Although she realized so many would one day reject this holy child of hers, she never allowed this torment to turn into wrath. Her supernatural love for God flooded into a motherly compassion for all humanity. She never stopped praying for the conversion of those who would participate in the death of the Lamb of God. Every one of us sinners has contributed to the passion of Christ. Every one of us sinners is loved immensely by the Mother of Christ.

Reflection

- Do we make sacrifices to God with little or great love?

- How special and valuable to us is the gift we offer to God?

- Do we hate sin?

- Does the sin of others wound us because of the unjust offense it gives to God?

- Are we sincerely dedicated to rooting out even the smallest of sins from our life?

- Do we make ourselves an offering to God in how we use our time, talents, and treasure?

- How well and often do we pray?

- Do we recognize prayer as our remedy, our medicine, our strength, our weapon, our refuge of peace, and our answer to the question of darkness?

THE FLIGHT INTO EGYPT

The poverty of the Holy Family is probably experienced more in this suffering than in others. Christ was born in a stable, yet they have even less than a stable now. It was a difficult journey in those days to travel a far distance with very few preparations. They probably had little or no food, shelter, or supplies to alleviate their hardship. It must have been a surprise to awake in the middle of the night and flee one's own land, especially for such a small group—one man, one woman, and a small child. The cold, hunger, and the unknown all may have weighed profoundly on the heart of Mary. However, these are the easiest of her trials.

Although our Lady trusts perfectly in God, she very well may have suffered for the sake of Saint Joseph, whose job was to secure and provide for the needs of his wife and child. Mary's sorrows never clouded her inclination to empathetically accompany others in their turmoil. She loved her spouse greatly and sought to help him fulfill his obligations to the Holy Family. If the weight of his obligation pressed upon him, it pressed upon her as well.

The Holy Family not only leaves their home and culture but also their place of worship. They leave behind the temple, the place of Mary's adolescence, where she grew in knowledge and holiness, the place of sacrifice and adoration of God. Yet she fled with the New Temple, the Body of Christ. Such suffering our Lady must have experienced, knowing that God Almighty was not even accepted among His own people. How many years has God prepared the Israelites to recognize the Messiah? Instead of being accepted and exalted, the Messiah is hunted by King Herod and those under his charge. Herod thirsts to put to death the Creator of life.

When God became man in the incarnation, He crowned humanity by uniting it to His divinity. Without understanding the full effect of their actions, man tries to destroy the most beautiful part of all creation—the humanity of Jesus. This must have been a lasting and deep revelation of the hideousness of sin for our Lady. Who could want to hurt this most special child? She understood better than any other the value of His life and the wisdom of God's plan of salvation. Her love for Christ grew every day, which only allowed the evil desires of man to pierce more deeply into her sinless heart.

The Blessed Virgin was inundated with sorrow as she realized the torment of the mothers who lost their firstborn sons in Bethlehem. The Holy Family fled from the terror of Herod as he sought to kill the King of Kings. Regardless of the many miles that separated them from the infanticide, Mary heard the cries of those mothers and felt their devastation. Their torment was simply a foreshadowing of her impending detriment. These children, called the Holy Innocents, were the first to lose their lives because of a hatred for Christ.

An old pious tradition relays a story on the journey to Egypt. The Holy Family took refuge one night in a robber's cave where they met a woman and her child who was leprous. After the woman gave water to the Blessed Virgin to bathe the infant Body of Christ, she then used the same water on her leprous son, and he was healed of his leprosy. This little child was Dismas, the repentant thief who was crucified with Christ. As water cleansed his leprosy of the body in infancy, so the Blood of Christ cleansed the leprosy of his soul in adulthood. Although the historicity of this story is uncertain, it does provide an example of the poetic beauty of God's providence.

Because the Holy Family flees their people and land, Christ is raised in a pagan land. This was the land from which God freed the Israelites from slavery, famine, peril, and death. Rather than raise Jesus in the land God promised to their ancestors, they must live in the land where their ancestors toiled under four hundred years of slavery. Everyone around them fails to acknowledge the One True God. They are surrounded by idol worshipers while God walks among them.

The Egyptians' indifference toward Jesus was certainly an acute and hidden anguish for Mary. How many times did she smell the incense or burnt flesh offered to a false god while carrying in her arms the Almighty? How many gods of clay and stone were the object of the Egyptians' praise while the living God passed by hidden in human flesh? Clearly, her suffering was not confined to the flight alone but the entirety of their stay in Egypt. The length of this stay is unknown. Some think two years; others say many more. Consequently, the length of this sorrow is also unknown.

Only growth in holiness helps give us a glimpse of the depth of her suffering caused by the sins and indifference of the people against her Son. As we advance spiritually and enjoy a more fervent love for God, we also become more sensitive to every sin against Him. The unique holiness of Mary increased her sensitivity to each sin she witnessed. She observed the Savior as an outcast among the people He desired to save. She did not only see but also felt the indifference with which He was treated. So, she continued to pray for their hearts to be softened and their souls converted.

Reflection

- Do we trust God?

- Are we easily removed from the peace God offers by our sorrows, disappointments, and struggles?

- Is the unknown a source of greater trust or a source of temptation for us?

- Do we really believe that God does not give us more than we can handle and that He provides for all our needs?

- Are we more offended by an offense against ourselves or a direct offense against God?

- Are we able to set aside our turmoil to help others in their turmoil?

- Do we desire the salvation of others?

- Do we put forth effort in our own spiritual lives and in the world around us to aid others in their relationship with God?

- As we grow spiritually, we encounter other defects, stronger temptations, and more difficulty. These should only aid in our continued sanctity.

THREE DAYS LOSS

The men of Israel were required to come to Jerusalem three times a year for various religious feasts to comply with the Jewish laws of worship. Mary and Jesus may have only accompanied Joseph for the Feast of Unleavened Bread. This Feast correlates to our Easter celebration, the highest feast of the liturgical calendar. These journeys were often made in caravans for the purposes of security and convenience.

The third sorrow of Mary concerns a three-day period in which Jesus remained in Jerusalem while Mary and Joseph began the journey back to Nazareth. Though it may seem impossible for a man and woman who love their son dearly to embark on a journey without knowing his whereabouts, greater historical context clarifies the separation. One possibility of His disappearance concerns the structure of these caravans. The men and the women traveled in the same caravan but separately. The men traveled with the men, and the women with the women. Therefore, Mary and Joseph may have been under the impression that Jesus was with the other. Regardless, what is certain is that God allowed this occurrence through which Mary was immersed in great agony.

A mother desires to be near her son; a disciple desires to be near her teacher. In a single instant of realization, the Blessed Virgin was left without her perfect Son and her supreme teacher. The absence of Jesus was for her the absence of breath. This sorrow is often considered by the spiritual authors of old as the most painful for Mary in a certain sense. Her insight into the interior life of Christ was second to none. As she grew spiritually, her insight grew in clarity. However, the light of her clarity was eclipsed by the torment of confusion in this dolor.

She did not understand how or why this happened. How tumultuous were her thoughts while she anxiously traveled back to Jerusalem and scoured the city in pursuit of Christ? Where was He? Why was He gone? Did she do something wrong? Was His death coming so soon? Had He returned to the Father before the redemption of man? Would He come back to her? Without food and rest, Mary and Joseph searched for the Savior.

Likely, the most painful element of this sorrow was that Jesus chose to stay behind. Knowing the torment it would cause them, He remained in Jerusalem to aid those in need, to beg for bread, and to discourse with the scholars in the temple. Our Lord chose not to say a single word to them or send an angel to inform them. He allowed them to be cast into doubt and darkness when He could have prevented it. Despite all her grace and her knowledge, Mary was cast into the darkness of confusion and the unknown. Nevertheless, she accepted all of it. God's will be done. This distance between her and Jesus forces Mary to experience the effect of sin. Separation from God is a direct effect of sin. Although she did not commit any sin, she was not prevented from encountering certain effects from it. She was always in perfect union with God because of the grace she received at her conception and the blameless way she lived. She never tasted the fruit of disobedience like Eve, but she tasted the effects of it. Mary demonstrates a likeness to Christ because He also blamelessly endured these effects though He remained purely innocent.

Finally, after days of tireless travel and ceaseless searching throughout Jerusalem, our Lady hears the voice of her Savior and sees His countenance again. This moment brought a tidal wave of alleviation to her troubled mind. Yet our Lord's answer to her question only renewed that recently alleviated trouble. When she asked Him why He had done this to them, He responded, "How is it that you sought me? Did you not know that I must be in my Father's house?"[19]

Father Faber notes:

He [Jesus] has taken out Simeon's sword [from her heart] and thrust in His own. Why had Mary sought Him? Oh, think of Bethlehem, the wilderness, Egypt, and Nazareth! Why had she sought Him? Poor Mother! Could she have done otherwise than seek Him? How could she have lived without Him? There were a thousand reasons why she should have sought Him. Does He deny her rights? Is He about to take them from her, and just, too, in the finding of Him? Rights! They were His own gift. He could take them back if He pleased. But His Flesh, His Blood, His beating Heart, were not these in some sense hers? No! Rather hers were His.[20]

Reflection

- How sharply do we feel the distance between us and God?

- Mortal sin causes a true and complete separation; do we run back ceaselessly and tirelessly until we find a confessional?

- Are we filled with anxiety, sorrow, and concern until we are restored to Christ?

- How sharply do we feel the distance caused by our venial sins and imperfections?

- We are able to slowly, almost imperceptibly pull away from Christ by our attachments to worldly pleasures. How well do we remain vigilant over our spiritual lives?

- How hard do we work to overcome our defects, vices, and attachments?

- How dangerous these are because we can begin to feel satisfied with what the world offers. A real danger in the spiritual life is to seek satisfaction in anything or anyone other than God. Truly, it must be an outrageous offense to God when we have attachments because, in some way, we diminish the manifestation of the infinite glory of God by comparing Him to some finite thing or some human person.

ENCOUNTER WITH JESUS ON THE VIA CRUCIS

Although this dolor may seem to be no different than any other moment of the passion of our Lord, the Church has selected it intentionally. A lifetime of anguish is endured in the moment Mary and Christ encountered each other on the way to the cross. Time must have stopped for them. The quantity of mutual love, mutual knowledge, mutual understanding, mutual surrender, and mutual resolve must have been inexpressible. How many times had both foreseen this passion in their personal prayers and meditations? Finally, it arrived, and she discovered that the pain was not lessened by foreknowledge.

How many blasphemies, how many outrages, how much abuse, how much torture, apathy, and evil surrounded her Son? Not even all the love and insight our Lady possessed allowed her to fully grasp the splendor of God; yet here He was, the object of such hideous inhumanity. Saint Catherine of Genoa had to be supported by God lest she die when God allowed her to see the true malice of even a single venial sin. Jesus carried the weight of all sins. The Immaculate Heart was pierced by every syllable and every action of sin against His Majesty. How many times can a single soul be pierced? How many pieces can a heart be broken into before it ceases to beat?

The Most Sacred Heart of Jesus and the Immaculate Heart of Mary are so united that it is more proper to consider them as one heart. Therefore, in this encounter between them on the way to the cross, each of them could see their own heart before them. Both were ravaged by pain, both were carrying an almost unbearable cross, both were in the deepest levels of suffering; yet this encounter increased their sorrow.

Our Lady's suffering peaked, knowing that she was, at that moment, one of the greatest causes of His suffering. Christ's knowledge of the depth of her sorrow was an exceeding torment that greatly increased His agony.

Father Faber notes:

And behold! She was one of the numbers [one of those adding to the weight of the Cross of Her Son, not for her sins but by the sight of her own sufferings]. She was adding to His load. She was more than doubling the weight of that heavy cross He was carrying. The sight of her face at the corner of that street had been worse a thousand times than the terrible scourging at the pillar. It was her face which had thrown Him down upon the ground in that third fall.[21]

Like the third dolor taught us, wherever Christ was, our Lady needed to be. How could she not seek Christ those three days of His absence, and how could she not be near Him during His most difficult hours of suffering and death? Regardless of the suffering that emerged from this encounter, she would not be absent from Her Savior. She would allow Him once again to look into her soul, this island of holiness amid an abyss of sin. Whatever forms of terrible torment into which He would enter, she would follow.

Another element of her sorrow includes her inability to console Him while others with evil intentions drew near to harm Him. The flesh they flagellated came from her womb; the Blood they spilled formed in her body; the face they beat was the face from which she could barely stand to remove her eyes for over thirty years. Anguish drowned her soul for the crimes of those persecuting Jesus. So much she desired their salvation, those whose sandals stepped in the Blood of her Son, whose words were like javelins to her heart. Even then, and even more, she pursued their salvation.

This is the first dolor our Lady faced without the support and presence of Saint Joseph. How comforting this humble, loving, and holy man was to the suffering heart of our Lady for so many years! He was a rock of piety and humility who comforted her to the best of His ability. Now, the reality of his passing was felt perhaps even more acutely than the moment he breathed his last.

Finally, only our Lady could understand and appreciate the acute agony that tore through her Son's Sacred Heart as a result of the apostle's absence. John was there, but where were the others? That sharp knife cut so deeply the Most Sacred Heart, and consequently, it also split open the Immaculate Heart. How many times did our Lady try to draw Judas away from the path of sin? She lost one of her little ones to the enemy, the ancient serpent whose enmity with Mary was foretold from of old. Jesus is not the first son she lost. Judas abandoned God, betrayed her Son, and ostensibly refused repentance. These ancillary realities added no small quantity to her sorrow because they added no small quantity to the weight of Christ's cross. The Son of God descended from His celestial throne to find His lost sheep. Stubbornly, some refuse to be found.

Reflection

- How quickly are we willing to be absent from our Savior because of suffering?

- How much pain does it cause us when we sin against Him when we realize we are the source of His suffering?

- Is the road we are presently traveling leading to greater holiness? Or must we honestly acknowledge that we are less virtuous and less holy than last year or the year before?

- How well do we carry our cross?

- How quickly do we complain about its weight or the duration of the journey? Mary did not look to lessen her sorrow; she sought to please God and save souls through her sorrows. Let us not forget, we are a cause of our Lady's sorrow because we are a cause of our Lord's passion.

Father Faber notes:

> Thus, the fourth dolor contains within itself the whole science and mystery of cross-bearing. This is the wisdom we learn from the picture while we gaze on Mary in the streets of the cruel Jerusalem. The eye of her soul sees the fair-haired Boy in the Temple, whom she sought more than twenty years ago, while her bodily eye is fixed on the pale and bleeding and earth-stained Man, going with sound of trumpet and

the chorus of earth's curse to His doom. And shall we, who gave Him that heavy cross to bear, and kept weighing it after we had given it, as if our cruelty were not satisfied, refuse to bear the sweet grace-giving crosses which He binds on us, so little too as when we have borne them for a while, we are forced to confess they are [indeed so little]? Oh, no! Let us do now as Mary did then, — look at Him who is on the road before us and see how the beauty of the Sacred Heart sits with meek majesty and attractive love on the woe-worn disfigured Countenance.[22]

THE CRUCIFIXION AND DEATH OF JESUS

The scene of the crucifixion bore striking similarities and dissimilarities to the birth of Christ. He was laid on the wood of a manger in a place called the "house of bread"—Bethlehem. At the crucifixion, He was laid on the rough wood of the cross to be the Bread of Life for all. As an infant, He was naked and clothed by Mary; now He was stripped of the garments she made for Him. She crowned Him with her kisses; they crowned Him with thorns. God made Himself vulnerable and hidden in the flesh of an innocent child; God's glory is hidden in the torn flesh of an accused criminal. In Bethlehem, even the animals acknowledged His majesty; at the crucifixion, even the high priest demanded His death. Our Lady honored the hands and feet of our Lord in the manger. Now, His hands and feet are pierced with nails and fastened to a cross on Mount Calvary.

Each time the hammer made contact with the nail, a new wave of sorrow washed over the heart of Mary. Each cry of the nail echoed through her soul. Each strike sent a frequency of absolute anguish through His Body. Father Faber notes the falling of the hammer was not one event; rather, each knock of the nail was a "separate martyrdom."[23] Having premade holes in the wood that were further apart than Christ's wingspan, they had to stretch Him by pulling a rope until the sound of His dislocating shoulder was heard by all who gathered.[24] Those were the arms that embraced her and the hands that served her. How many times had she seen Him cure illnesses and remove sorrows through the touch of His hands? How many miles did she walk with Him as He exhausted His feet in pursuit of souls throughout the land? She watched as those same arms were stretched to injury and the same hands and feet were desecrated by sin.

Our Lady was submerged deeper into her unbearable sorrow as the mockery of her Son amplified. Men casting lots for His garments demonstrated a disregard for human life and common decorum. Pious tradition relays the possibility that the garment He wore was originally made by Mary in His infancy. This special vestment grew with Him throughout the years and kept its integrity. Therefore, it was like the garments and shoes of the ancient Israelites, which Moses recorded as not having been worn out and destroyed by use.[25] The seamless garment representing the One, Holy, Catholic, and Apostolic Church is now to be won in a game of chance by those who crucified Christ. Is this not the garment through which the woman with the flow of blood was healed? Is this not a most precious relic worth more than all gold? These pearls of great price are cast before swine.

In these long hours on the cross, the only refreshment she tasted was the conversion of the penitent thief. What wonderful relief, as imperfect of a relief as it could have been, for her who could see at the same time both the horrific cost of this soul's conversion (namely the terrifying death of her Son) and the joy of its effect. In direct contrast to this slight refreshment, Mary's sorrows were amassed when the impenitent thief proved unmoved by the slaughter of the Lamb of God. How many graces, how many attempts from his guardian angel, how many opportunities he had to repent but would not. For the salvation of souls, our Lord dies. For the salvation of souls, our Lady suffers with Him, yet this man only a few feet away refuses the perfect love flowing from the wounds of Jesus. "Mary saw his eternity before her as in a vista. She took in at a glance the peculiar terror of his case. There came a sigh out of her heart at the loss of this poor wretched son, which had sorrow enough in it to repair the outraged majesty of God but not enough to soften the sinner's heart."[26]

Mary witnessed her Son give perfect adoration to the Father every moment of His agony. She watched Him grow colder, whiter, heavier of breath as death drew closer. Did the amount of blood that flowed seem endless as the Mercy purchased by His Blood is limitless? Jesus suffered far more interiorly than exteriorly. However, the sufferings of His heart were visible to the eye of His Mother. She knew the consolation of God that was kept away from Him. She knew the havoc our sins made in His soul. She knew the constant strife He endured within Himself.

Even in this hideous death, she was drawn closer to her Son. Were their hearts ever so alike as when they were both torn open for the love of each other? Again, we must consider how Mary's suffering added profoundly to the sufferings of Christ. In fact, some contemplatives claim that moments of Christ's attention to the sorrows of Mary caused such grief that all other sufferings were eclipsed. Although their hearts were as but one, they were reciprocally an instrument of torture for the other.

For the remaining years of her life, Mary must have heard these words of Christ sound repeatedly throughout her soul: "My God, my God, why have you forsaken me?"[27] These words echo the words of Psalm 22 which describes the terrible torments encountered by the cruelty of human enemies. It's not a repudiation of God, but a plea for His aid. It's not an accusation against His Father, but a recognition that life and salvation are in His hands. These words spoken by our Lord are a mystery that serve as a rich source of meditation on the interior torments He faced at the hands of His cruel tormentors. Christ's soul must have trembled at the countless and terrible sins of humanity for which He offered Himself. What extensive sorrow flooded His soul at the countless men and women who would refuse the salvation He merited in His death. However, it is not correct to assume that God the Father abandoned His Son or poured His wrath on Him. God the Father never lost sight of the innocence and purity of His Son. The sacrifice of Christ and the redemption He offers to man is a sacrifice of love, a free gift of obedience, not a punishment the Father forced on the innocent one in place of the guilty. For love of humanity, the Father allowed the Son to offer Himself for us when He willed our salvation. For love of humanity, the Son gave Himself over to His assassins. The Father was and is ever-pleased with His Son's perfect and loving sacrifice; Jesus Christ is never separated from the Father. Nevertheless, our Lady must have held these words of the cry of her Son in her heart; she must have felt their weight and measured their meaning more keenly than any other. As Christ announced the abandonment of the Father, Mary abandoned herself to the will of the Father perfectly.

The death of our Lord marked a universality of suffering for Mary. Who can number the variations of sorrow, the degree of anguish she felt in those three hours? What fiber of her body was not exhausted? What fiber of her faith was not tested? What fiber of her soul was not pressed by the intensity of this mystery? Next to the cross, she remained firm in faith, supported by grace, and stood near her Son. She never collapsed nor surrendered under the weight of her cross. Our Lady manifests the strength and help of God in the direst situations. She makes it visibly clear that she also stands near us in our trials; she is always present to offer the support we need. God be praised!

Reflection

- The sword of Simeon found its target in the crucifixion of Christ. The death of Christ is the crucifixion, the passion, and the martyrdom of Mary. Saint Anselm remarked, "Whatever cruelty was exercised upon the bodies of the martyrs was light, or rather it was as nothing, compared to the cruelty of Mary's passion." Although we cannot ever fully grasp, or even remotely so, the true extent of Mary's sorrows, we must continue to penetrate this mystery more deeply through regular meditation and prayer. The torment described is the cost of sin.

- Who could ever have imagined that the taste of the forbidden fruit would be the root of such tragic pain?

- Who could ever have guessed the cost of sin, which we commit regularly, is so high?

- How well do we confess our sins? At least in theory, are we willing to endure great pain, lose a child, be humiliated, or rejected, and lose our career for the sake of not committing even a single sin intentionally?

- Do we exalt wealth and possessions more than the love of God, thereby casting lots with the soldiers at the foot of the cross?

- Do we "preach Christ crucified" with Saint Paul through daily mortification?

- With how much acceptance, love, and goodwill do we bear our cross?

- In what ways do we use our sufferings for greater conformity to Christ?

- This is the way we console Him.

- Sin, in its hideousness, nearly eclipsed the beauty of God on the cross, yet the love of Jesus and Mary made even suffering, darkness, and death beautiful. God acting through us can make even our ordinary daily woes something precious and turn them into a crown of everlasting glory in heaven. Mary suffered in silence.

- Do we cultivate silence?

- How else can we be united to God's will?

- Silence is the language of God, the voice of heaven, and the medium in which the Holy Spirit breathes and moves. Mary's silence at the cross is a glorious hymn of love in the ears of the Almighty.

THE BODY OF CHRIST TAKEN DOWN FROM THE CROSS

Through the humanity of Christ, salvation is offered to the world. His Body, fastened to the cross, hangs lifeless as the signs of death become more apparent. The soldiers fail to grasp the value of His death and the honor they owe to the Body of Christ. Sacrilegiously, they thrust a spear into His side to confirm "it is finished." The sacrifice is complete. To see the condition of the Body of Christ, which came from her virginal womb, treated with such irreverence wounds her as if the spear were thrust into her own side. The Holy Mother witnessed the jolt to the Corpse and heard the sound of His flesh torn open. The shock of this maltreatment sent a fresh wave of sorrow that permeated the entirety of her being.

Our Lord is the unblemished Lamb; therefore, His legs were not to be broken like the other two men who died with Him. Rather, His heart was pierced; water and Blood flowed. This Most Sacred Heart was opened to all who would enter. "Knock and the door shall be opened."[28] The opening of this Heart is the beginning of the opening of the gates of heaven. Blood and water are the liquids of life and salvation. Both are essential for natural life on earth. Both are essential for eternal life. The water of Baptism is the first of the seven sacraments. The Blood of Christ, the Eucharist, is the summit of the Christian Faith because it enriches our union with Christ. The entire life of the Church is found between these two holy liquids. Even after the Word of God is separated from His human Body, God still feeds His sheep with it. This Blood and this water shower the Roman soldier who callously impales the Body of His Savior. At this moment, the Roman soldier's heart is also pierced, not with a spear, but with the fruit of our Lord's sacrifice. The soldier was ensuring that Christ was already dead, but he caused eternal life to pour from His side. His spear was changed by the Heart of Christ into a key that opened the gate of heaven. His spear poked a hole in the floor of heaven, and salvation poured into the world. The soldier is one of a vast multitude of souls to be saved by these two same sacred fluids. This imagery is but a brief glimpse into all that occurred in this sorrow. Our Lady experienced every tormentous element; nothing is hidden from her love.

As the men began to incrementally free the limbs of Jesus, Mary was handed the instruments which attached Him to the rough wood of the cross. She held the very nails that held His Body to the tree, the tools used to make this common cross the new Tree of Life. She felt the hardened metal, the size, and weight of each nail. She did not only see the effect of these instruments in the hands of sinners, but she also held them in her sinless hands as well. She was without Her Son, who bore a Heart that was perfectly in union with hers. Each passing moment brought a greater realization of the emptiness of life without Christ. Loneliness, a certain characteristic of the sixth dolor, ravaged her interior life and flooded her experience.

Consider the deep imprint on the memory of Mary that must have been made as our Lord's limp and life-less Body was slowly taken down from the cross. She gave Him that Body and the flame of human life which animated It. Sin snuffed it out. She alone understood its true value. She was elevated above all other human persons when granted the responsibility to develop and nurture this same Body in her own womb. Therefore, the responsibility to care for this brutalized Body is left to her. Her loneliness is magnified by the weight of this responsibility. How many times for the remaining years of her life did she replay this same image in her memo-ry, in her contemplation, and in her prayers? How long she must have taken to cleanse and prepare His Body for burial. Did she receive the crown of thorns, or did she remove them from Her Son's head herself? Did she count the holes made by the numerous thorns? Did any of those thorns that pierced Jesus pierce her as she was removing them? How many rags were necessary to clean only the beaten and unrecognizable face of our

Savior? How much of His holy Blood was rung from His soaked hair? She replaced the patches of flesh that were barely hanging to His Body. She saw the exposed ribs which concealed the heart which pumped salvation to the world.

The tender love our Lady expressed in preparing Christ's Body far surpassed the wretched hatred expressed in putting His Body into that state. The tender love with which our Lady treated that sacred vessel of the second Person of the Holy Trinity was greater than the love of all the other saints combined. Nothing came so close to a just reparation for the offenses against our Lord than the love of His Mother.

There is a real connection between the lifeless Body of Christ and the Blessed Sacrament, which gives us eternal life. Did she have a vision of all the ways that her priests, her special sons, would mishandle the Eucharist in the future? Did she see how many of them would consecrate the bread and wine in the state of mortal sin, or how many would "eat and drink judgment" upon themselves through sacrilegious Communions?[29] How was it that our Lord gave Himself over to the brutal Romans? How is it that our Lord still gives Himself over to us unworthy Christians in Holy Communion?

Reflection

- Mary is a model for us in times of sorrow. She is near the one who suffers. She suffers with us. Do we suffer with others?

- Do we use our sufferings as a worthy and holy oil to anoint the Body of Christ?

- Do we grow in greater love of God by our sufferings, or do they cause us to turn inward and wallow in self-pity?

- How does this dolor aid us in our participation at Mass? It is the real and true sacrifice Jesus made present to us.

- How does this dolor affect our own worship of God truly present in the Eucharist? We must continually strive to prepare our souls, minds, bodies, and hearts to receive Him worthily and well.

- Do we warm the coldness of our hearts and strive to renounce the distractions of our minds before and while receiving Him? As precious was the lifeless Body of Christ after His death, so much more valuable is the Holy Eucharist. His Body was not united to His human soul or His divinity after His death until the resurrection on the third day. The Eucharist, however, is the Body, Blood, Soul, and Divinity of Jesus Christ.

- Are we willing to delay our daily duties to spend a few minutes before the Eucharist where we can accompany the Blessed Virgin in adoring our Savior?

THE ENTOMBMENT OF THE BODY OF JESUS

Father Faber reflected, "It was when she left the tomb her first homelessness began."[30] The strain of leaving behind the Body of Christ in the belly of the earth was a devastating source of anguish for Mary. She had already suffered from the lack of sleep, the lack of food, and the strain on her body caused by the long passion of Christ. The sorrow of Mary outreached even the knowledge of the angels.[31] The culmination of the previous sorrows finds its full force in this dolor. At least, in suffering with Christ during His passion, He was near. She either had Him or His Body present to her. This sorrow left her empty, silent, and without consolation. O how she would have preferred to die with her Son if it were the will of God. In no way did she desire anything contrary to His will at any moment; however, to suffer with Him was easier than to suffer without Him.

There is much resemblance between this sorrow and the third. Again, she found herself torn away from the very center of her existence. She was left without any consolation and any way of dampening the anguish of the sword's penetration. "There is no darkness like a world without Jesus . . . the absence of Jesus is, as it were, a participation in the most grievous pain of hell."[32]

Although the third is generally considered the greatest of her woes in a sense, she at least had someone to search for. In this sorrow, however, she had nowhere to go, nobody to seek, and no duty to perform for her Son. In the third, there was an ignorance that God allowed to overtake her. She did not understand why Christ remained in Jerusalem; however, in the seventh, she knew all of it. She knew where He was and why He was gone. How does it feel to be beyond the reach of consolation?

In the last sorrow, she still had obligations to Jesus by caring for the tattered remains of His Body. As the great stone closed the entrance to His tomb and separated her from the Body of her Son, her increasing loneliness spilled over into desolation.[33] He was her home, her life, and the center of her existence. No food could give her the necessary strength to carry this burden. No house could shelter her from this storm of devastation. No companionship could save her from this isolation. For one who is fully devoted to God, the world offers no remedy or calmative that can pacify the soul.

The correlation between the seventh sorrow and the infancy of Jesus increases the bitterness of Mary's agony. She laid His Body and fixed the burial garments just as she had laid Him in the manger and swaddled Him with clothes. Did she make for Him the burial garments as she had made for Him the garment with which He was swaddled? Her joy was complete as she gazed upon her Son in the manger. Her sorrow was complete as she gazed upon Him in the tomb just a few moments before leaving His Body behind.

Mary was surrounded by reminders of Jesus, which prevented any moment of solace. The disciples of Christ who became more like Him throughout their years of discipleship reminded her of her Son. She remembered Jesus by the presence of Saint John, the compunction of Saint Mary Magdalene, the preaching of Saint Peter, the stories of their miracles. Father Faber states, "Her whole being was drenched with bitterness. The swords in her soul reached every nerve and fiber in her frame."[34]

Yet through all this torment, she remained the source of consolation to Saint John, Saint Mary Magdalene, Saint Peter, and many others. The measure of grace and beauty in her soul was unmatched and nearly un-measured. During all this evil and all the sufferings that flowed over her heart, she never lost the smallest mea-sure of kindness. She never lost the slightest amount of compassion for others. Not a single drop of the ocean of selflessness that resided in her soul evaporated. She was already perfectly fulfilling her role as the Mother of all Christians despite the ineffable pain caused by being the Mother of Jesus.

Reflection

- Are we tranquil in the tumult of anguish?

- Kindness in our sorrows is a medicine of consolation for us. How willing are we to accommodate others even when it is hard?

- Sorrow often causes people to think only of themselves and only of loss. Mary gives us the method of Christian suffering.

- What or who is it that we love most in this world? Is it God? Do we use our difficulties as a justification for our self-love or an instrument for greater true love?

- Self-pity is a very destructive weapon of the enemy. It teaches us to draw the attention of others to ourselves. It gives us an excuse to waste time and to be distracted from the will of God. Sword after sword penetrated the Immaculate Heart of our Lady, but she never wavered from God's will, she never abandoned her service to others, she never counted the cost. She left the tomb to continue Christ's mission.

STELLA MARIS

Star of the Sea

When thou seest thyself upon the stream of
time, tossed between wind and wave, rather
than treading upon the firm earth, look up to
the Star: call, 'Mary!'

When pride, or ambition, or calumny, or
envy, like the wild waves, toss thee hither and
thither, look up to the Star: call, 'Mary!'

When thy heart, with anger, or sinful desires,
is whipped about like a little ship in a tempest,
then look up to the Star: call, 'Mary!'

When the greatness of thy sins affrights thee,
or the horror of thy conscience makes thee
ashamed, and thou beginnest to feel thyself
in the grasp of despair, as in a whirlpool,
dragged down and down into the abyss, then
look up to the Star: call, 'Mary!'

In danger, in anxiety, in doubts, think of
Mary, call on Mary: let her name be ever on
thy lips, let it always abide in thy heart.

But to win her intercession, depart not from the pattern of her life. Only follow her, and thou wilt never go astray; call upon her, and thou wilt not despond; think of her, and thou wilt not falsely judge. If she takes thee by the hand, thou canst not fall; if she protects thee, thou canst know no fear; under her guidance thou wilt never weary; with her favor thou wilt be landed happily. So mayest thou learn, in thy own self, how true it is what is written: 'And the name of the Virgin was Mary; that is, Star of the sea.'[35]

Endnotes

1 "He [the son of David, ultimately speaking of Jesus] shall build a house for my name, and I will establish the throne of his kingdom forever." (2 Samuel 7:13. The Holy Bible. Revised Standard Version; Second Catholic Edition. San Francisco: Ignatius Press, 2006.) "But you, O Bethlehem Ephrathah, who are little to be among the clans of Judah, from you shall come forth for me one who is to be ruler in Israel, whose origin is from of old, from ancient days." (Micah 5:2.)

2 Isaiah 53:5–6.

3 Luke 1:28–33.

4 Luke 2:35.

5 "I will put enmity between you and the woman, and between your seed and her seed; he shall bruise your head, and you shall bruise his heel." (Genesis 3:15.)

6 "And the angel said to her, 'The Holy Spirit will come upon you, and the power of the Most High will overshadow you; therefore the child to be born will be called holy, the Son of God.'" (Luke 1:35.)

7 Leen, Edward. *The Holy Spirit*.

8 *Ineffabilis Deus*.

9 "But those that were sown upon the good soil are the ones who hear the word and accept it and bear fruit, thirty-fold and sixty-fold and a hundred-fold." (Mark 4:20.)

10 "Now I rejoice in my sufferings for your sake, and in my flesh I complete what is lacking in Christ's afflictions for the sake of his body, that is, the church." (Colossians 1:24.)

11 Faber, *The Foot of the Cross, or The Sorrows of Mary*, 66.

12 Faber, *The Foot of the Cross, or The Sorrows of Mary*, 50.

13 Faber, *The Foot of the Cross, or The Sorrows of Mary*, 64.

14 Faber, *The Foot of the Cross, or The Sorrows of Mary*, 106.

15 Luke 1:38.

16 Faber, The Foot of the Cross, or The Sorrows of Mary, 128.

17 "and Simeon blessed them and said to Mary his mother, 'Behold, this child is set for the fall and rising of many in Israel, and for a sign that is spoken against

(and a sword will pierce through your own soul also), that thoughts out of many hearts may be revealed.'" (Luke 2:34–35.)

18 Faber, *The Foot of the Cross, or The Sorrows of Mary*, 107.

19 Luke 2:49.

20 Faber, *The Foot of the Cross, or The Sorrows of Mary*, 221.

21 Faber, *The Foot of the Cross, or The Sorrows of Mary*, 282.

22 Faber, *The Foot of the Cross, or The Sorrows of Mary*, 320–321.

23 Faber, *The Foot of the Cross, or The Sorrows of Mary*, 325.

24 Faber, *The Foot of the Cross, or The Sorrows of Mary*, 325.

25 "Your clothing did not wear out upon you, and your foot did not swell, these forty years." (Deuteronomy 8:4.)

26 Faber, *The Foot of the Cross, or The Sorrows of Mary*, 332.

27 Matthew 27:46.

28 Matthew 7:7.

29 1 Corinthians 11:29.

30 Faber, *The Foot of the Cross, or The Sorrows of Mary*, 445.

31 Faber, *The Foot of the Cross, or The Sorrows of Mary*, 447.

32 Faber, *The Foot of the Cross, or The Sorrows of Mary*, 488.

33 Faber, *The Foot of the Cross, or The Sorrows of Mary*, 462.

34 Faber, *The Foot of the Cross, or The Sorrows of Mary*, 20.

35 Lasance, *Our Lady Book*, 291.